MIND ELEVATION:

A Guide to Improving Your Mental Diet in 30 Days

DR. JOHN C. TYUS

ISBN-13: 978-1729777916

ISBN-10: 1729777910

Cover Design: majesticcreativity.com

BRING DR. JOHN TO YOUR

EDUCATIONAL INSTITUTION

Contact Dr. John today and begin the conversation!

www.drjohntyus.com

CONNECT WITH US:

Facebook: /drjohntyus

Instagram: @drjohntyus

Twitter: @drjohntyus

INTRODUCTION

Habits are acted out on a daily basis in our lives. Many of those habits and thoughts are done subconsciously. Many of us have habits that are unhealthy and cause us to live life at a lower level than we deserve. At times breaking those habits are difficult and take consistent effort. In order to break negative habits you must create new positive habits. This book was designed with the intent to feed your mind positive information on a daily basis, aided with action steps that will encourage healthy thinking and application. Just as we eat healthy food to be physically healthier, we must consume healthy mental thoughts so we can live healthier lives mentally.

This book will inspire, inform and challenge you to elevate to your next level of positive thinking and living.

Included are Mental Elevations in the areas of:

- How to finish what you start
- The importance of forgiveness
- Why having the right relationships are important
- Why you must not allow your past to limit your future
- How to build the right team
- Why standing out is important
- How to overcome the challenges of life
- How to turn your passion into action
- How to embrace your voice

The hardest thing about our goals is starting them, and the 2nd hardest thing is finishing them! Be a finisher!

@drjohntyus

Most people in life remain dreamers and never graduate to the place of doing. While you are on your journey of life remember that your dream will only become yours if you run after it. Dreams don't just fall into your lap. Dreams are things that need to be chased and pursued. In addition to starting and pursuing your dream you must finish the course. In life I've discovered that consistency is one of our biggest issues. Some start but little finish! Are you a finisher?

DAY 1: ACTION STEPS

- Write down 3 ideas or goals on paper you wish to achieve
- Write down how you plan on achieving that goal or steps you need to take to make it happen
- Write down the time frame in which you wish to achieve the goal
- START NOW!

LAZINESS AND PROCRASTINATION WILL KILL YOUR PURPOSE

@DRJOHNTYUS

The reason you were created is your purpose. Discovering that is not always the easiest thing. At times it takes a lot of bumps in the road until you discover it. Your purpose is often discovered in your area of gifting but we have 2 killers waiting to snatch it away from you. "Procrastination" and "Fear" are the 2 killers of your purpose. Don't let them rob you ever again. It may be your grades, it may be your business but these 2 killers try their best to rob you of your God-given purpose. Those that procrastinate don't view what they are doing as important but set themselves up for a future of self-gratification rather than purpose-gratification. Don't be lazy with your life because you are the ONLY one in control of the outcome. Love yourself enough to do the things you need to do now so you can enjoy yourself later.

DAY 2: ACTION STEPS

- Realize what causes you fear and mentally make a choice to resist it
- Decide today to walk in FAITH and BELIEVE you were created to do great things
- Sit down and make weekly action steps to move towards your goal and purpose in life
- Learn to make the RIGHT decisions quickly. The more you think about it the more you leave yourself the option to talk yourself out of doing what is right

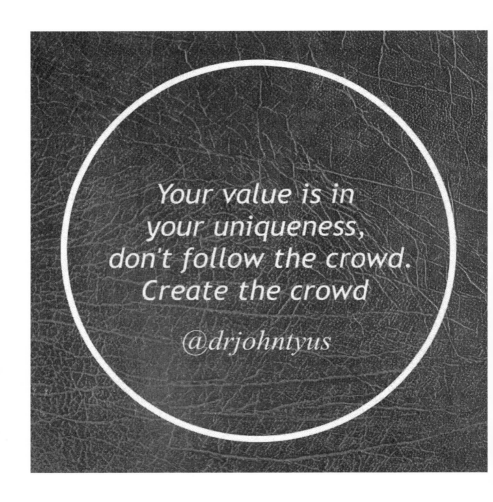

Your value is in
your uniqueness,
don't follow the crowd.
Create the crowd

@drjohntyus

The mistake that many people make is that they try to be everyone else but themselves. It is crucial that you learn to BE who you are and confident in that space. There will be many people and things that will try to pull you in the other direction but your worth is found in your uniqueness. What makes a diamond so valuable isn't its beauty, but its rarity. The rarer you are the more valuable you are. The only way to make that happen is for you to strive to be you and no one else.

DAY 3: ACTION STEPS

- Don't compare yourself to anyone else. You were created to lead not follow
- Write down the things that make you different and read it 3 times today, out loud, to yourself
- Take 10 minutes today to focus on yourself, areas you need to improve, and write them down. Understand that progression is a process and doesn't happen overnight

The more YOU respect
YOU the more others will
respect YOU. We teach
others how to respect us
by how we respect
ourselves.

@drjohntyus

People who respect themselves will only engage on a personal level with people that respect them. Their tolerance level for misbehavior is limited and when they sense people that don't respect them they remove themselves from the situation. When you respect yourself you also respect your time and realize that any and every one can't use it. Individuals that respect themselves hold themselves to a higher standard and are focused on their dreams and goals. People sense those who are focused and are less likely to try and distract them.

DAY 4: ACTION STEPS

- Make a conscious effort to not allow people to disrespect you by making sure you respect you
- Separate yourself from those friends and connections that do not respect your growth
- Create a list of 3 moral standards that you will hold yourself to and walk them out daily

There are many things
You want to do in life
Because there are many
Things you were created
To do!

@drjohntyus

Have you ever wanted to do many things in life and had the problem of choosing just one? This is a big concern for people. The answer is: you were created to do many things in life. The challenge is you must choose 1 to 2 things to focus your energy. You have to ask yourself these 4 questions: Which ones do I love the most? Which ones bring me the most joy and happiness? Which ones am I naturally good at? Which one, if I had the choice, would I do for the rest of my life? Begin to invest in yourself concerning your top 2 passions through reading material and watching videos. This will build your knowledge base around your passion. Down the line you will most likely find your other ideas being connected to your top 2 and will begin to work in those areas as well.

DAY 5: ACTION STEPS

- Take time out today to write down a list of things you are passionate about

- After writing them down, pick out the top 2 that bring you the most joy and where you have a natural ability

- Spend 15 minutes a day on each of your 2 passions learning about them, whether that be watching videos, reading about them or talking to others who are involved with it

Don't accept a good thing
and miss out on the right thing!

@drjohntyus

In life one of our biggest mistakes is that we are so anxious for the RIGHT thing that we accept a GOOD thing in its place. Know your worth and your value and never settle until you discover the Right thing. Good things look very similar to the right thing and can be very misleading if you are not focused. Life will hand you many Good things but will hand you few Right things. Know the difference. Trust your gut instinct and be honest with yourself. In my experience the majority of the time our gut feelings are correct. Do not override them because of your desire. Wait it out and be patient. Time reveals all things.

DAY 6: ACTION STEPS

- Take a moment today and think about your relationships. Are they GOOD or RIGHT?

- Concerning your goals and dreams in life are you putting forth GOOD effort or the RIGHT effort

- Make a conscious choice to be patient and wait on RIGHT things instead of settling for GOOD

DON'T SEEK VALIDATION
SEEK AUTHENTICITY

@DRJOHNTYUS

Seeking validation from others only leads to seeking more validation. What people are seeking in life is not validation but rather significance and meaning. Significance doesn't come from seeking people to affirm you, but rather comes from those that seek to be authentically themselves. The world is filled with others seeking to please and be liked by others.

True value comes from those who are originals and are okay with it. You will face many temptations to follow the crowd and forsake your originality, don't! Your true impact, wealth and effectiveness in life will come from you being authentically you.

DAY 7: ACTION STEPS

- Take time today and write down 7 things that you love about yourself
- Make a declaration statement in the mirror *"I am good enough, I am valuable, and I am unique"*.
- Next *"Read out loud the 7 things that you love and wrote about yourself"*
- Today, seek out opportunities to encourage your originality by not being afraid to respectfully express yourself and what you feel

Character is proven in how you respond to FIRE!

@drjohntyus

If you are reading this, you've experience hardships in life. You may be young but you've still tasted the sting that life has to offer in some form. The problem is we have viewed hardships as a negative instead of a positive. Negative times come for 2 reasons: to plant a positive seed as a response and to show you where you are. Do you handle things right or do you respond emotionally and regret it later? Your character is proven in your response. View it as an opportunity to show how strong your character is.

DAY 8: ACTION STEPS

- Take a moment and think about a tough situation and look at how you can become better from it
- Look at that same situation and see how you can respond in a positive manner
- As you go through your day you will be faced with many temptations to do wrong. Do the right thing and watch good things return back to you

If you can conquer
YOU
You can conquer your
DREAM

@drjohntyus

27

Our biggest test in life is not obtaining our dreams; the biggest test in life is conquering you. More often than not in life the ENEMY is not the ENEMY the real ENEMY is the INNER-ME! Conquering the real dragon in life which is the pain of our past and our mindset is the real test. We have all been programmed by our environment to blame others for our lack of attainment. Your dreams are easy to obtain the moment you overcome the mentality that you can't obtain them. More often than not we talk ourselves out of our own dreams. You must believe that you can and be willing to fight for that belief. Then your dreams will seem easier to obtain.

DAY 9: ACTION STEPS

- Take a moment today and write down your dream life in the next 10 years
- Write down what you need to accomplish every year to reach that 10 year goal
- Write down things that you feel would get in the way of making this a reality
- Write down ways to overcome those challenges that may try to stop your dream from happening
- Put the paper in a place you can see often and daily remind yourself of your commitment to your dream

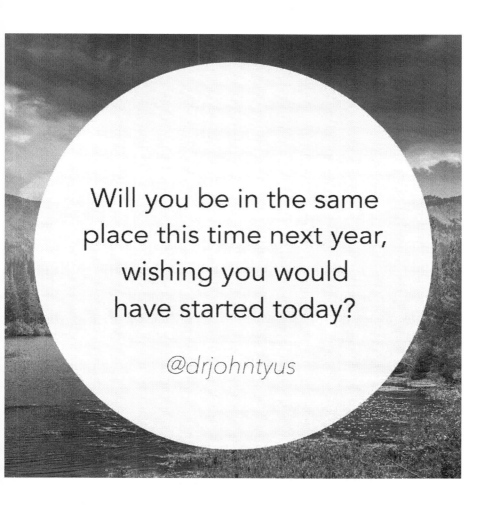

Will you be in the same place this time next year, wishing you would have started today?

@drjohntyus

Procrastination is one of our biggest setbacks to our progression and pursuit of our dreams. The *"I will get to it later"* mindset proves to never be profitable in your life. Life will continue to happen and if you continue to put off your dreams and goals you will be bombarded with new situations to conquer before you make the step. Time waits for no one and it will pass you by whether you are ready for it or not. Many people are still dreaming about things they could have obtained and conquered years later. Don't allow the ancient enemy of dreams called procrastination to rob you of time!

DAY 10: ACTION STEPS

- Write down a plan on how you will be different this very time next year. This can include your schooling, business, relationships, spiritual life or physical health.
- Make a weekly plan on how you will move and progress towards those goals; DON'T WAIT

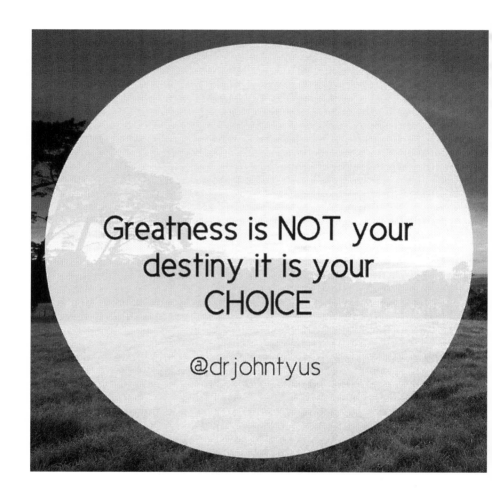

Greatness is NOT your destiny it is your CHOICE

@drjohntyus

Many people will argue with this quote because they believe it is already written in time that greatness is your destiny. I believe we were all created to be great and do great things in our specific area of talent but achieving that is left up to the individual. Depending on how hard you work towards your goals depends on the amount of success you will see from them. Mentally you have to make a decision to NOT fail! Everyone is born with potential but few realize it. Take control of your life and make the right choices!

DAY 11: ACTION STEPS

- Make the choice to be great. Greatness is reserved for those who choose it

- Make the small choices today that will impact your journey in a positive way. Greatness is found in the details of life

- Choose your friends wisely. Socialize with greatness, learn from those that are great and apply what they do to your own life. Becoming great also depends on the company you keep

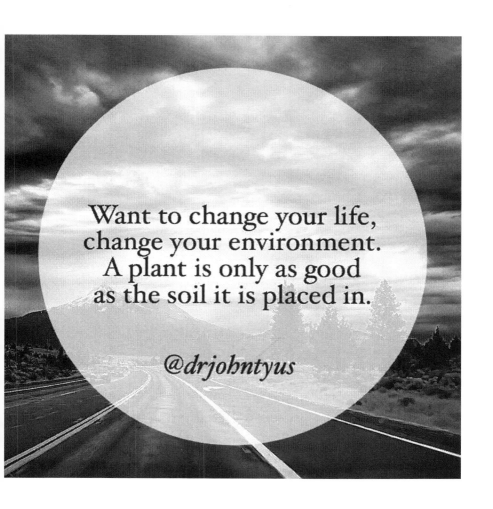

Want to change your life,
change your environment.
A plant is only as good
as the soil it is placed in.

@drjohntyus

36

A plant's entire existence depends on the environment where it is placed. If the soil it is placed in doesn't receive proper nutrients the plant will die. Like the plant our life depends on the environment we are placed in and the people we are around. It is important that you choose the right friends as you go along on your journey. The company you keep will either tear you down or build you up. We as people are easily influenced. Make sure if you are going to be influenced it is by the right thing and the right people. If you are not growing in life one of the reasons to consider is your environment.

DAY 12: ACTION STEPS

- Make sure your friends have a focus in life and are just as driven in life as you

- Make sure if you add anyone to your life that they are strategically there to cultivate you or there for you to help cultivate

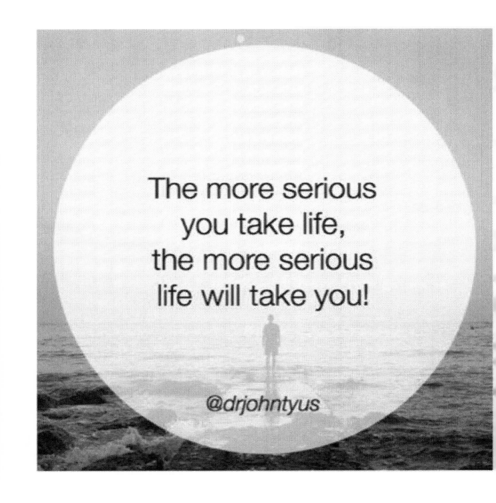

The more serious
you take life,
the more serious
life will take you!

@drjohntyus

39

Life is given as a gift to us all. We should take it seriously. The longer you play with life the more time you waste. In reality none of us know when our lives will end. It is important we honor the gift of life and treat it with care. Life is here for us to enjoy it but also to be intentional concerning it. Life is precious. Some individual's lives are shorter than others. Make sure you embrace it. The funny thing about life is what you put in is what you will get out. The more serious you take the time you have the more good time will be to you. Invest in your knowledge, invest in helping build others, invest in relationships and watch the blessings of those things return back to you.

DAY 13: ACTION STEPS

- Take a moment today and enjoy your current season of life. Good or Bad it is teaching you
- Do not be so concerned with tomorrow that you can't enjoy today. Learn to live in the moment
- Write down 5 things you are truly grateful for in life
- Read them 3 times and make a choice to KNOW you are blessed

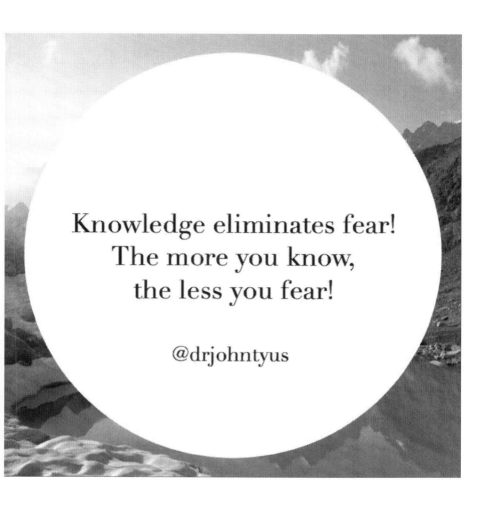

Knowledge eliminates fear!
The more you know,
the less you fear!

@drjohntyus

In my years of speaking and mentoring I've learned that one of the main reasons people experience fear is because of the lack of knowledge. The old acronym F.E.A.R. *(False Evidence Appearing Real)* is in fact true. The realty is if you know the real evidence in place of false evidence you have the ability to rise above fear. Fear comes to control you through ignorance, but you can put fear in its place the more you learn. The more aware and knowledgeable you become the less you leave room for fear.

DAY 14: ACTION STEPS

- Take a moment today and read an article concerning the area you are most fearful about. The article should speak to ways to overcome that area of fear

- Watch a motivational video that gives tips on how to conquer that area of fear in your life

- Begin to apply the thoughts and tips you read to your life

We are so busy wearing other people's names that we never wear our own

@drjohntyus

Billions of dollars are spent annually on apparel each year. The concept that people would rather wear, be connected to, or liked by those that we believe hold value is limiting. As a child I remember the better name brand clothing and shoes you wore the greater your popularity. I was not searching just for clothes that were popular. I was searching for acceptance and significance. Today it is less about clothes and more about social media. Realize that social media is simply what others want you to know about them and rarely shows the reality of who they are.

Most people post just receive "likes" but they rarely "like" themselves. Love yourself, like yourself and at that point you will wear you instead of wearing someone else.

DAY 15: ACTION STEPS

- Take a moment today and realize you are valuable not because of what you wear but because of who you are
- Look at your social media accounts and take assessment of what you post for yourself or post for others
- Take a 6-hour break from social media; cleansing yourself for a moment and connect with the real world

Forgiveness doesn't free the other person, *It Frees You.*

@drjohntyus

Forgiveness is one of the keys to living a healthy life. Many individuals are sick, bitter and unhealthy because of holding past pains. Contrary to belief, forgiveness is not for others it is for you. Each one of you have experienced past pains and mistreatments. It is important that you not allow that to negatively affect your living experience. Allow it to make you "better" not "bitter". The problem with people that are bitter is that they make even sweet situations sour. Life is amazing when you are able to live life without anger and bitterness towards others. Don't allow anyone to rob you of your freedom. Forgive and be free!

DAY 16: ACTION STEPS

- Ask yourself *"Who in my past have I not forgiven that have done wrong to me?"* *(Be Honest)*

- Write their names down on a piece of paper; say out loud I forgive ____ *(their name)*. When the pain wants to reenter your mind quickly say I forgive them and that you are free from the pain

FALL IN LOVE
WITH THE WORK,
NOT THE RECOGNITION
OF THE WORK.

@DRJOHNTYUS

51

Some of our biggest issues in life are trying to win other's approval. Even at times we work for all the wrong reasons. Often times we do it simply to be recognized and seen by others which only increases our desire for attention. The moment you fall in love with the work itself, is the same moment you become at peace because your intent is pure. Pure intentions always produce peace. Your intentions become pure thus allowing the work to flow easier and seamlessly.

Believe it or not people can often tell who is working for the purpose of the work or the purpose of attention. When your motive is the work itself that provides energy to keep going when times get tough because you are focused on the mission and not the attention.

DAY 17: ACTION STEPS

- Ask yourself *"Why do I do what I do?*

- Ask yourself *"Is my motive the mission or attention?"*

- If you find yourself to be more selfish, don't be too hard on yourself. Many of us have been there, but begin to make intentional effort to do things for the right reasons ONLY

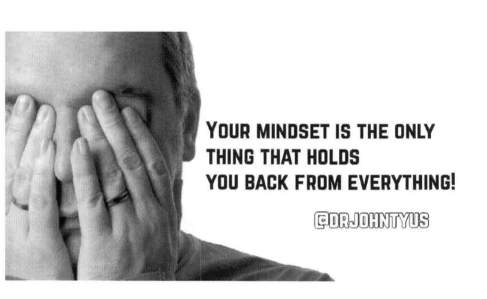

YOUR MINDSET IS THE ONLY THING THAT HOLDS YOU BACK FROM EVERYTHING!

@DRJOHNTYUS

In most cases where you are today is the result of your belief system. There are thousands of books that discuss the power of your mind and how you have the ability to change your situation once you believe. Dreams come true only to those that believe they are possible. Nothing is possible until you believe it is. Life is filled with storms that come to shake your self-belief system. While the storms of life may leave, the impression it has on our minds is often still there. We need to find healing. Not from the storm itself but from the impressions the storm has left on our minds. All things are possible only if you believe.

DAY 18: ACTION STEPS

- Ask yourself *"What is holding me back from true fulfillment in life?"*

- Ask yourself *"Have I let go of the negative impressions my storms have left on my mind?"*

- If these are you, challenge the thought and make a CHOICE to be free and think the opposite

Watch your words!
Many are dealing
with curses they have spoken
over their own lives.
Speak
LIFE!

@drjohntyus

I'm sure you have seen those horror movies that speak about curses being on individual's lives. You have seen how people respond in fear knowing they are cursed. Well this is true in more ways than people believe. We curse ourselves by what we speak from our mouths. My favorite book speaks about life and death being in the power of the tongue. We spend much of our lives cursing ourselves, speaking negativity over our own lives and wonder why our life turns out the way it does. You have the power to speak life over yourself. The more life you speak the more your mind will believe. The more your mind believes the more your life will comply with your belief.

DAY 19: ACTION STEPS

- Begin everyday speaking "I WILL" statements about you.

- Affirm yourself and build yourself

- Speak Life! Go 1 day just speaking positive things and avoid ALL negative talk and thoughts

You can't have self esteem
without first having
self awareness. You
can't esteem
something
you don't
know

@drjohntyus

The biggest issue in life comes from a lack of understanding yourself and knowing who you are. You are not what you own or what you wear but your value comes from who you were created to be.

Criminal activity comes from a place of not knowing. Not knowing who we are and our value in society causes us to mismanage our gifts. This is why drug dealers are often great at business. They have skills of understanding profit margins and appealing to their customer's needs.

This is why we should not misplace our gifts and who we are. The moment you discover who you are no one will ever be able to tell you otherwise. There is a confidence that comes with self-discovery. A light clicks on in your soul and you are no longer control by other's opinions but you become your own person. If you want to build you, find you first! You cannot build something you don't know.

DAY 20: ACTION STEPS

- Make an effort not to follow people that are not going places. Self-discovery is a process and does not happen overnight. In the process of following good leadership you will begin to discover who you are
- Connect with people that know themselves and eventually you will as well.

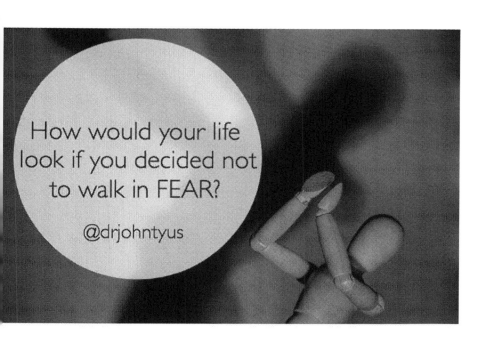

How would your life look if you decided not to walk in FEAR?

@drjohntyus

My favorite teacher the late Dr. Myles Munroe stated, "The wealthiest place on earth isn't the gold mine of South Africa, or the Middle East where you will find oil, it is the cemetery. It is there you will find dreams that never became a reality". One of the main enemies to your purpose is FEAR. It was created to keep you away from maximizing your potential and realizing your possibility. Everyone will have their own personal fight with FEAR. It wears many different faces and looks different to different people. Once you conquer fear endless possibilities become reachable.

DAY 21: ACTION STEPS

- What would you do if you decided not to walk in FEAR?
- Whatever your answer was that is exactly what you must do to put FEAR in its place
- Write down your top 3 FEARS on a piece of paper
- Write down 3 ways to overcome those fears or face them
- Tear up the piece of paper with the FEARS on it and declare out loud "Fear Won't Control Me"

The higher the tree the deeper the root, if you want to go higher you must dig deeper. @drjohntyus

On nature shows it is common to see trees that are so large that they seem to reach to the sky. The tallest tree in the world is said to be the redwood and are said to easily reach 300 feet tall. Just as tall as these trees are they are just as deep underneath the ground. In many cases their roots are deeper than the tree is tall. Just like these trees it is obvious what happens on the outside but it is more important what is taking place on the inside, underneath the surface. If you wish to go higher in life, your roots including your morals, ethics and character should be the most important pieces in your developmental journey.

DAY 22: ACTION STEPS

- Take a moment and think about your roots and how strong they are

- Are they strong enough to sustain your dreams and goals? If not,

- Begin to focus on doing the right things by others for the right reason. This will strengthen your roots and foundation for where you are going in life. Life will challenge you in these areas consistently but you must prove how strong your roots are

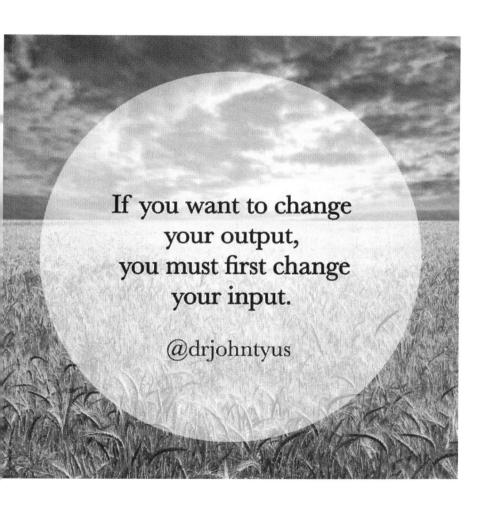

If you want to change
your output,
you must first change
your input.

@drjohntyus

Many people ask, *"Dr. John, how did you change your life?"* My response is always *"I changed my diet"*. My life changed once I decided to put something else inside of me. We cannot produce anything that we don't put inside of us first. That is like asking a man to make a withdrawal from his bank account without first putting any cash inside the bank. If you desire to be different and be better you must put different and better inside. My father would always say, *"You can't change and still do the same thing"*. This is true if you desire a better life you must consume better things.

DAY 23: ACTION STEPS

- Make an effort to listen to one motivational video a day. This will change your mental diet
- Trade your music, friends, social media outlets for more positive versions of the same things

The gift within you
is always greater
than the struggle
that surrounds you

@drjohntyus

You were born with something great within you and were made to overcome every challenge and battle that life throws your way. Many of you reading this are dealing with issues in life that you are not comfortable speaking about.

Today I want you to know that whatever you are faced with you were created to overcome. An old Jewish saying is "The race isn't given to the one who is fastest or strongest but to the one who can last until the end". This means that our job in life is to outlast each season life throws our way.

In life we are given four seasons: winter, spring, summer and autumn.

Each one brings a different feel and serves a different purpose, but none of them last. In the seed of each   season lies another.

DAY 24: ACTION STEPS

- Whatever struggle in life you face today remember it is only temporary. Outlast it!

- Even our hard seasons have their purpose and work for us.

- Keep Going! A new season is coming!

The choices you make today will reap the fruit of tomorrow

@drjohntyus

Everything that we are living today is directly connected to what we have planted in times past. Changing our thinking pattern from a survival mindset to an investor mindset will cause us to live more fruitful lives. The investments I'm referring to aren't real estate or the stock market but rather your personal development. The more you invest in you today the more fruit you will reap tomorrow. When planting seeds the gardener doesn't see the fruit right away but must continue to invest into the land by watering the seeds, making sure it gets proper sunlight and nourishment. The gardener knows if they put in the work now they will reap the fruit later.

Your education, relationship building, spiritual development or personal

developments have nothing to do with now
but everything to do with later.

DAY 25: ACTION STEPS

- Water your developmental seeds consistently knowing you will reap great fruit later
- Set goals for the next year of your life
- Write a monthly plan how to attain those goals
- Search for a book that will feed your mind and your dream. Begin reading

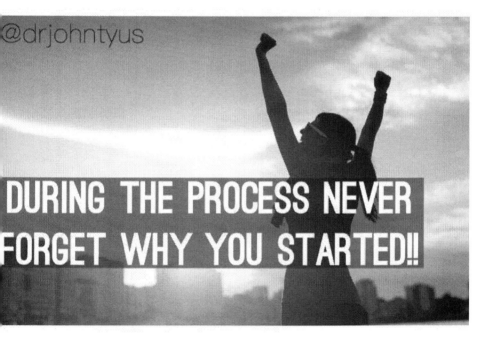

@drjohntyus

DURING THE PROCESS NEVER FORGET WHY YOU STARTED!!

The most important question to ask yourself is "WHY". We know what we want to do but if we don't have a clear reason "why" it will always fall through somewhere in the process. Knowing why will keep you focused and keep you going when things get rough. Rough times come to prove if your "WHY" is strong enough. The stronger your "WHY" statement is the harder it will be to distract you from the goal. Whatever journey you are on right now you started for a reason. Remember why you started and that will fuel you to keep going.

DAY 26: ACTION STEPS

- Think about your vision and goals and write down on a piece of paper your "WHY" statement

- Post this piece of paper in a place where you can look at it often to remind you in the hard times why you started. This will serve as a reminder for you why you must keep going

Success in life depends on your will to attain it. Your will is a function of your mind. Once you are convinced that what you are living isn't good enough and make up your mind that you want change, your life will change. We have a desire to change but few people actually have the will to do so. When you are willing to change, it becomes easier to change certain habits that produce negativity and undesirable life outcomes. The moment you are ready to change and willing to fight for it, you will begin to change your life's diet. This includes evaluating relationships and friendships that are not productive, things you watch and music you listen to because you understand the concept of production. You cannot produce anything you don't put inside of you first. So if you want positivity in your life, you will change your diet to only positive things.

DAY 27: ACTION STEPS

- Include in your daily diet a motivation/inspirational video in the morning to help start your day
- Reduce music that speaks on negative things and begin listening to positive music

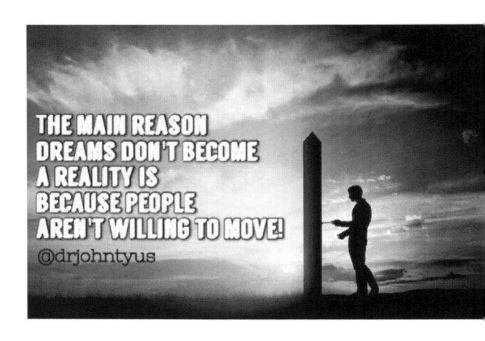

THE MAIN REASON
DREAMS DON'T BECOME
A REALITY IS
BECAUSE PEOPLE
AREN'T WILLING TO MOVE!

@drjohntyus

The truth of the matter is that we as people give up WAY TOO EASILY on our dreams! An overwhelming number of individuals give up on their dreams before they are ever reached. It isn't the fact that we don't have the ABILTY to conquer our dreams but we lack the WILL to do so. Have you ever heard of the saying *"Where there is a will there is a way"*? This statement is true. In fact you will never discover your "WHY" without your "WILL". The way leads to your why in life but must first begin with your will. The real question is "Are you willing?"

DAY 28: ACTION STEPS

- Take 5 minutes and think about the self-sabotaging thoughts that have stopped you from reaching your dreams
- Write them down!
- Tear up the piece of paper and never go back to it again
- Write down all the reason why you DESERVE your dream.
- Put it on your wall to look at every day. This will keep your "will" motivated and inspired

Work a job that will
fund your vision,
until your vision
funds your life.

@drjohntyus

The key to this quote is to first discover your vision, because without a vision you walk around life aimlessly and without a guide. Your vision serves as your compass in life and will keep you focused when distractions arise in life. Fulfilling your dream doesn't come easy or cheap. Often times our jobs serve as a means to produce income only to fund our vision in life.

If you stay true to your vision and dream, eventually your job will become your vision. You will inspire enough people that you will be able to live off of your dream.

DAY 29: ACTION STEPS

- Make a monthly budget by looking at your income and expenses
- Set aside some money that solely goes towards fulfilling your vision
- Understand that your job serves as preparation for your dream.
- Don't forsake small beginnings but rather take each day as it comes and over perform at work. This will produce work ethic

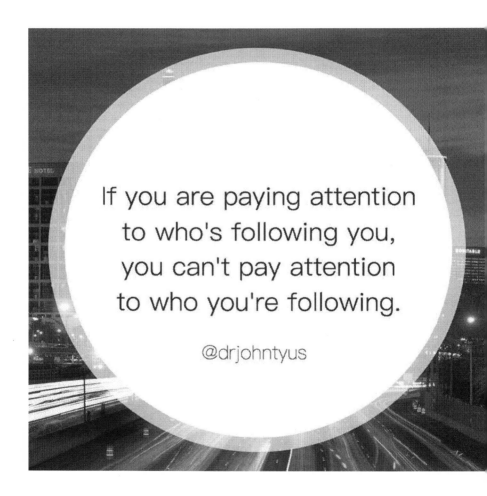

If you are paying attention
to who's following you,
you can't pay attention
to who you're following.

@drjohntyus

A lesson to learn is that your value doesn't come from who is following or paying attention to you. Many people will pay attention to you for the wrong reasons. Many individuals' motives are not pure and often pay attention to see what you are doing wrong rather than what you are doing right. Be careful of these people.

Make sure you are following good examples of individuals who are proven, tried and true. Mentorship is the highest call of leadership. Make sure you are aware of who is in front of you rather than who is behind you. We reflect who we follow.

DAY 30: ACTION STEPS

- Take a moment and seek out who you are following in life
- Seek for mentorship that is positive
- Once you discover someone that you are interested in learning from, ask if you could spend some time and shadow them as they work

BRING DR. JOHN TO YOUR

EDUCATIONAL INSTITUTION

Contact Dr. John today and begin the conversation!

www.drjohntyus.com

CONNECT WITH US:

Facebook: /drjohntyus

Instagram: @drjohntyus

Twitter:　　@drjohntyus

Dr. John C. Tyus
Award Winning Speaker,
Author, Life Strategist

Dr. Tyus has earned a Bachelor's Degree in Business Administration with a dual minor in Marketing and Management from Franklin University, attained his Master's Degree in Pastoral Counseling from Liberty University and earned his doctorate degree from United Theological Seminary where the title of his dissertation was *"Designing a Mentoring Program for Fatherless Black Males in a Post-Modern Generation"*.

Dr. Tyus founded a mentoring and leadership development program entitled *"The I.D. Movement"* aiming to *Inspire* and *Develop* fatherless young men into positive male models for their families and communities. The I.D. Movement has now branched into community

97

conversations and conferences.

A docu-series of the same name is currently in post-production with interviews from high esteemed individuals such as former Mayor Michael Coleman, Sunny Martin and Dr. Jamal Bryant.

Dr. Tyus is also a sought after inspirational speaker, lecturer and presenter, having spoken to thousands of youth and young adults across the nation. He has presented to high schools, colleges, churches, leadership conferences and nonprofit organizations across the country. He has been recognized for his work by The Ohio House of Representatives and was the recipient of The Dr. Martin Luther King Jr. Social Justice Award of Ohio for his work in advancing social change. He has been referred to as one of his generation's best speakers and leaders. The model he lives by is a slogan from his favorite author and teacher the late Dr. Myles Munroe and that is to *"live full, die empty"*.

NOTES

Made in the USA
Coppell, TX
23 October 2019

10349820R00069